Developing Leaders with A Passion For Kingdom Work

Benny L. Dozier, Sr.

Developing Leaders With A Passion For Kingdom Work

ABLE Publications

ISBN 978-0-9885463-0-1

Dedication

First, I would like to thank you Holy Spirit for your leadership. You are awesome and I want to thank you for inspiring me to write this book. I would like to thank my little lady and wife Prophetess Gerry, who I believe is the epitome of what a leader should be and for pastoring Power and Light Church of Gary for 13 years. I want to thank my mother Ada Dozier who has exemplified what leadership is all about in my life. I want to thank my family for your love and continued support. I want to thank my staff Pastor Carolyn, Lady Cathedral, Deaconess Jennifer and Deaconess Tinakka. I would be remiss if I didn't thank my 2nd man Apostle Darence for all the support he has given me as an awesome leader. I'd like to thank my spiritual father, Elder Leo for 30 years of imparting wisdom and giving me timely revelation from God over the years. Thank you Power and Light Ministries and the A.P.I.N. for your support. I love you all.

I would like to dedicate this book to my friend and mentor Apostle Joseph L. Stanford, for launching me out into the apostolic both nationally and internationally, and to my friend Apostle James Randolph for the prophecies that have kept me on course, and also to my longtime friend Pastor Eddie Barnes for great friendship over the last 30 years.

TABLE OF CONTENTS

Introduction

Introduction

This book deals with an area of ministry that I have a great deal of passion for – leadership. My desire is to give a clear understanding of why leadership is so vital in the 21st century and why God has a double standard when it comes to leaders versus lay members within the Body of Christ.   I believe the Body of Christ is not lacking titles, such as bishops, prophets, watchmen, teachers, etc. or using different phrases such as, 'five - fold ministry' or 'apostolic'. I do believe the body is lacking a great understanding of what leadership is and the application of the principles that are foundational to the making of great leaders. I believe that the oil flows down as Psalm 133 states.   I like what John Maxwell says: "Everything rises and falls on leadership".

When I speak of developing leaders with a passion for kingdom work, I am referring to the fact that every leader has a process, and that process consists of life situations (jobs and workplace, family, you and your own personal development or the need for development) -all the facets of life that we experience that help us grow, develop, and mature into the individuals and leaders God has destined us to become. I believe the process God used in the making of Moses consisted of all of these. His process entailed educational training, dealing with family (although he wasn't raised with his biological family), marriage, parenting, spending 40 years in Egypt, and spending another forty years working with Jethro in learning what it means to be subordinate (Exodus chps. 2-3). The ultimate goal was for Moses to be a leader that would be used in the forefront - the process necessary in becoming the leader who would ultimately lead God's people out of Egypt.

When we talk about a passion for kingdom work, I must look back and reflect on much of the training I've received while attending Wagner Leadership Institute. We must understand that the Church must make the transition from the Gospel of Salvation (The Evangelistic Mandate, Mark 16:15-16) to the Gospel of the Kingdom (The Kingdom Mandate, Matt. 28:19) This transition doesn't exclude the saving of souls or the gospel of salvation, but incorporates the concept of discipling nations. The premise is that if we can transform a nation, then we can win the souls in that nation.

The vision and passion that a senior leader has along with what God has placed in his or her heart as it relates to God, God's people, and God's ministry must be transferred from the senior leader to others that are like-minded. The same anointing that was on Moses God said He would take it and place it on the seventy elders:

"Then I will come down and talk with you there. I will take of the spirit that is upon you and will put the same upon them; and they shall bear the burden of the people with you, that you may not bear it yourself alone" (Numbers 11:17).

Looking ahead to my next book on leadership, I'd would like to make some brief comments on the seven mountain mandate, which deals with social transformation and Kingdom work: I believe that there are leaders who will be or are already on the cutting edge, and are new *wineskins. These leaders are built for signs and wonders. These individuals will have the character and integrity to handle power, wealth, and influence, and **because of the passion they have for Kingdom work, they will make God known within the seven sectors of society as mentioned according to Revelation 17:9, Micah 4:4, and Isaiah 2:2. In case you are not familiar with these seven sectors of society, they are: church, family, education, government, business, media, and arts and entertainment.***

As you delve into this book, begin your journey with this prayer: Father, I pray now that everyone you lead through your Spirit, to read this book will receive a fresh download of present truth from you. May this present truth enhance their lives, that they will be blessed and you will be glorified. In Jesus' name, Amen.

Enjoy!

Chapter 1

What Is Leadership?

Leaders are made and not born. Leaders can be born with certain leadership qualities and even have the gift of leadership but they will still have to go through their God given process to become a leader and be developed into God's kind of leader. Just as one may be born a male, they must go through a process to become a man.

Leadership Is Influence

Leadership is influence, trust and respect. Influence is the act or power of producing an effect without a great deal of effort, force or direct command. In a leadership capacity, influence is the effect a leader has on those that are following them; how that leader can affect what people think, how they act, or respond. A leader will know when he or she has influence because people will begin to follow them.

Trust is to have confidence in something or someone. In order to trust others you must first trust God. When we trust God we can trust the God in others. Trust is what leadership is built upon. You can't build a team without first laying the foundation of trust.

Respect is a feeling or attitude of admiration toward someone or something. Respect is the highest level of leadership. It is a matter of leading - and not position, title or gender. Respect is something that is earned and not rewarded or demanded. John C. Maxwell said, "You must establish your own respect; no one else can do it for you. In other words, no one can tell someone or make someone respect you. If people don't respect you they won't follow you." If people don't like you they won't follow or trust you. When leaders gain respect leading becomes easier. You know you have influence when people begin to follow you but when leaders have respect, people continue following you. _Weak leaders believe that their position or title deserves respect. Strong leaders know that they must earn it._ Strong leaders understand the power of leadership – their lives are built on wisdom and revelation (Ephesians 1:17). Wisdom is truth learned in the past. Wisdom is what you have learned about God, yourself, and about the devil. Some people in leadership are trying to improve their lives as a leader by getting more revelation and knowledge of God's word.

Revelation has no strength or foundation without wisdom (Proverbs 4:7; 9:1, 3). Revelation is vital because it is present truth – it's what God is saying right now (II Peter 1:12). All leaders need to know what God is saying to the group of people or organization that they reside over.

A great example of gaining influence and earning respect would be in the case of David. David's father Jesse was not able to identify with David's leadership ability because of what his beliefs and views were in regards to what leadership is. Neither Samuel nor Jesse understood the process and criteria God wanted to use to choose this new leader. God rebuked Samuel concerning how the next king would be chosen. He told Samuel, *"Do not look at his appearance or at his physical stature, because I have refused him. For the* LORD *does not see as man sees; for man looks at the outward appearance, but the* LORD *looks at the heart" (I Samuel 16:7).* A great segment of the body of Christ chooses leaders based upon outward appearance- numerical growth of a ministry, name recognition, great intellect, or even who a leader may know in the political arena. None of these things are wrong, but God sees the heart of a man or woman, which is one of the most critical areas to be considered when it comes to that leader's influence over others or over themselves. David's brothers didn't have influence, but David did (I Samuel 16:18). A leader should already have influence before they are given a title or position.

In the seventeenth chapter of first Samuel, David took out Goliath. With this act of courage David gained the respect of his father. Years later, David gained influence over his father, brothers and other men who all came under David's leadership.

"David therefore departed thence, and escaped to the cave Adullam: and when his brethren and all his father's house heard it, they went down thither to him" (I Samuel 22:1).

In Acts chapter six the church needed seven more leaders to help the apostles carry out the assignments. The congregation was told to choose seven men of good reputation (Acts 6:3). They chose seven men they felt were capable of leading them because they trusted and respected these men. These men already had respect and influence within the congregation without having a title. The scriptures don't tell us specifically if any of these seven men chosen had titles or held positions because the essence of their leadership was the influence that they had.

"Finally, they must be well-respected by people who are not followers. Then they won't be trapped and disgraced by the devil... They must first prove themselves. Then if no one has anything against them, they can serve as officers" (I Timothy 3:7 & 10).

Can a leader have a positive influence over others without first having dominion over themselves? Having dominion over one's self is vital as it relates to being a leader and having influence over others. Apostle Paul talks about having personal dominion in Romans 6:9-14. These scriptures emphasize the fact that we must have dominion over our spirit, soul, and body, and we shouldn't yield our members to unrighteousness but yield them to righteousness that sin would have no more dominion in our lives.

Leadership is making tough decisions without compromising. Moses had to make a tough decision. Does he believe the two spies that had the vision or the ten who were entertaining the spirit of fear and their own deficiencies (Numbers 13:21-33-14:25). He yielded to the ten spies' observation of the giants in the promised land and the voice of the people instead of believing the two spies' observation of how fruitful the promised land was and what God had already told him about it.

I remember in 2006 in my own ministry when God told me to sell our church building and the parsonage. It was a very tough decision to make because we didn't have the consensus of the entire congregation. I believed God and the ones in our ministry that had the faith to trust the decision God had given me to make as the senior pastor. The end result was one of the greatest decisions I'd ever made. By selling those two buildings our ministry became almost debt free, and the new facility God blessed us to purchase is several times larger and helps us to fulfill the overall vision of our ministry in a much greater way.

Notes and Personal Reflection:

_____

_____

_____

_____

_____

_____

_____

_____

_____

_____

_____

_____

_____

_____

_____

Chapter 2

LEAD BY EXAMPLE

"Follow my example, as I follow the example of Christ" (I Corinthians 11:1).

What does your ministry represent? What does your ministry believe in? What is your ministry's mission/vision? The answers to those questions are what your leaders should represent everywhere they go. Leaders must lead by example. I tell my leaders that when I see them, I see myself. What this means is I accept and trust that they would lead as I would. Paul stated in I Corinthians 4:17, I am sending Timothy because he would give you what I would give you in Christ (paraphrased).

Leaders should be an example of what you and your ministry represent. Leaders must do what they say and say what they're doing throughout the ministry. Leaders should set the pattern for lay members to follow. They should be able to accept Godly challenges and rebuke in the areas of behavior, relationships, and finances. Leaders should be willing to give of their time, give their tithes and offering, and attend Sunday school, bible class, prayer services and all corporate worship services and classes that you have in your ministry.

> *When I see you,*
> *I see me.*

Lay members will do what they see their leaders doing and repeat what they hear their leaders saying. What leaders are doing unto God and for their ministry should spread like wildfire throughout the camp. Leaders should lead by their Ears and not by their Mouth. "He that has an ear let him hear what the Spirit of God is saying unto the Church" (Revelation 3:6). People follow leaders with a track record that is stronger than their own.

Deborah the prophetess was a judge (Judges 5:7). When Israel was in war the commander of Israel, Barak, stated that he wouldn't go into war unless Deborah went with him (Judges 4:8, paraphrased) This prophetess not only had a great deal of influence but she also had an awesome reputation and track record among the nation of Israel.

Leaders Must Know The Power Of Their Words

Naaman was able to receive healing because of the weight of his maid's words. Leaders must know how to bring a word to a senior leader! Likewise, a leader must know how to give the same word that his leader gives him to another leader. Elisha sent his messenger with a word for Naaman (II Kings 5:10). Elisha understood delegated authority on a level that Naaman did not because Naaman got angry because Elisha did not come himself. He listened to the maid, but almost aborted his blessing because he did not want to receive instructions from a messenger!

Leaders must be able to receive words of instruction and correction from elders. Elders must have the heart of their leaders as Jonathan's leader had his heart in I Samuel 14:7. Elders will say what the Pastor would say – that is the power of delegated authority.

> *Leaders should lead by their ears and not by their mouth.*

11

Words from people who are joined to you will sharpen you!

When leaders can keep God's word, keep their own word, and keep the corporate word, that leader's word will have substance and will sharpen you.

Leadership is developed over a process of time and not overnight. Leaders must understand what the will of God is for their lives! Leaders must understand what the purpose is concerning what they are facing, when they are facing it, without blaming others. When leaders react positively to trials, they glorify God, receive opportunities, and they develop integrity.

> *Leaders must keep God's word, their word, and the corporate word.*

W.W.W.G.T.

Leading by example involves being able to worship, warfare, work, and go through all at the same time with consistency.

"I heard your call in the nick of time; The day you needed me, I was there to help. Well, now is the right time to listen, the day to be helped. Don't put it off; don't frustrate God's work by showing up late, throwing a question mark over everything we're doing. Our work as God's servants gets validated—or not—in the details. People are watching us as we stay at our post, alertly, unswervingly . . . in hard times, tough times, bad times; when we're beaten up, jailed, and mobbed; working hard, working late, working without eating; with pure heart, clear head, steady hand; in gentleness, holiness, and honest love; when we're telling the truth, and when God's showing his power; when we're doing our best setting things right; when we're praised, when we're blamed; slandered, and honored; true to our word, though distrusted; ignored by the world, but recognized by God; terrifically alive, though rumored to be dead; beaten within an inch of our lives, but refusing to die; immersed in tears, yet always filled with deep joy; living on

handouts, yet enriching many; having nothing, having it all" (II Corinthians 6:2-10).

GREATER THE EXAMPLE GREATER THE FLOW!

God prepares leaders ahead of their time! God is looking for people who will fulfill the responsibility of "servanthood". We can never understand the responsibilities of leadership until we have served under the leadership of another. *"And if ye have not been faithful in that which is another man's, who shall give you that which is your own?" (Luke 16:12)*

Joshua served under Moses' leadership before he became a leader! Joshua had been strong in his position as a "servant" of Moses, so Joshua was being prepared by God to be the next leader after Moses' death.

"And Moses called unto Joshua, and said unto him in the sight of all Israel, Be strong and of a good courage: for thou must go with this people unto the land which the LORD hath sworn unto their fathers to give them; and thou shalt cause them to inherit it. And the LORD, he it is that doth go before thee; he will be with thee, he will not fail thee, neither

*forsake thee: fear not, neither be dismayed"
(Deuteronomy 31:7-8).*

*"Now after the death of Moses the servant of
the LORD it came to pass, that the LORD spake
unto Joshua the son of Nun, Moses' minister,
saying, Moses my servant is dead; now
therefore arise, go over this Jordan, thou, and
all this people, unto the land which I do give to
them, even to the children of Israel" (Joshua
1:1-2).*

**Elders and deacons must learn how to
pour water on their senior leader's hands!**
The bond between Elijah and Elisha was so
strong that Elisha walked away from his
natural parents and family position to follow
Elijah!

Elisha burned the twelve yoke of oxen he was
driving and forever left the fields because he
had found a surrogate father and a spiritual
mentor. When leaders learn to "pour water on
their senior leaders hands" they burn up their
plans, visions and agenda and learn to serve
the vision that their leader has!

Elijah knew that his assignment was being
completed down here on earth and Elisha
knew his spiritual father's time to depart was

near. He asked for a double portion of Elijah's anointing.

> *Greater the example,*
> *Greater the flow.*

"And it came to pass, when they were gone over, that Elijah said unto Elisha, Ask what I shall do for thee, before I be taken away from thee. And Elisha said, I pray thee, let a double portion of thy spirit be upon me. And he said, Thou hast asked a hard thing: nevertheless, if thou see me when I am taken from thee, it shall be so unto thee; but if not, it shall not be so" (II Kings 2:9-10.)

Elijah said to him that is a hard saying but never the less I will give it to you (paraphrased). When the whirlwind took Elijah to heaven his mantle fell upon Elisha which I believe was the legacy of the older prophet (Elijah) to the younger prophet. There's no true legacy without a true successor.

HAVING THE SAME SPIRIT

Having the same spirit as your senior leader keeps you teachable and always willing to learn. "A wise man will hear and will increase learning, and a man of understanding shall attain unto wise counsel" (Proverbs 1:5).

Having the same spirit as your senior leader means you love your local church, you feel ownership for it, but you understand that you are not the leader and you have a heart for it anyway. You have a love for the pastor and his or her spouse. You have insight and knowledge that you have gotten from your senior leader. You are fruitful, able to produce, and are helping to grow people within your ministry. You can mentor other leaders in the church, help bring them up, and teach them how to be joined to the senior leader and not to you.

Leaders having the same spirit as their senior leader will help that senior leader do what he or she feels God is leading them to do without stress. An example of this would be Jonathan's armor bearer keeping the stress out of their relationship. We can see that his heart was knitted to his senior leader's heart when he made the following statement with application, *"Do what you think is best, I am with you completely, whatever you decide"* (I Samuel 14:7).

Leaders must help carry the burden of ministry and not make it heavier. When a burden becomes heavier or more challenging within your ministry and the pastors, elders and other leaders don't have the same spirit as their senior leader, then they will increase the burden.

"I will take the Spirit that is upon you and will put the same upon them; and they shall share the burden of the people with you, that you may not bear it yourself alone" (Numbers 11:17).

PROBLEMS THAT WILL HINDER A LEADER

There are several things that could be mentioned in this section but I want to deal with one in particular – the sin of familiarity. **Familiarity occurs when leaders try to measure up to the senior leader, or they try to put him or her on the same level as they are on, or they think they see no difference between themselves and their senior leader**. I believe one of the ways the spirit of familiarity can enter a person's heart and mind is when they fail to honor their senior leader. *"Let the elders that rule well be counted worthy of double honour, especially they who labour in the word and doctrine" (I Timothy 5:17).*

I believe whoever you do not honor you will not value; whoever you don't value you will not protect. When you can value your senior leader, the revelation that he or she gives you will always keep you in proper alignment with that senior leader. This is one of the main reasons Jesus said, *"Verily I say unto you, No prophet is accepted in his own country" (Luke 4:24).* They did not honor Jesus as the son of God so they kept him at the level of only being Joseph's son. I teach those under my leadership that unless you honor, value and protect your senior leader you will never grow to the place where you can believe all and question nothing as me being your 'Jeremiah 3:15'.

An example of one who was operating under the spirit of familiarity was David's son Absalom. He was blessed to be his biological son and his spiritual son, but he failed to understand the power of honor. He allowed this spirit to try to usurp authority over David and the nation of Israel. He became insubordinate and the weight of power and influence caused his sudden death.

"And on this manner did Absalom to all Israel that came to the king for judgment: so Absalom stole the hearts of the men of Israel" *(II Samuel 15:6).*

And there came a messenger to David, saying, "The hearts of the men of Israel are after Absalom" (II Samuel 15:13).

The scripture tells us 'do not think more highly of yourself than you ought to' (Romans 12:3).

Aaron, Moses brother, also was influenced by the sin of familiarity. Aaron was Moses' mouthpiece and a priest, but when Moses left to be with God on the mountain of Mount Sinai to receive instructions from God Aaron stopped serving God and Moses by making them another "god". Aaron moved into the position of Senior Leader, he left his measure as "priest" by caring more about the people!

"And he received the gold from their hand, and he fashioned it with an engraving tool, and made a molded calf. Then they said, "This is your god, O Israel, that brought you out of the land of Egypt!" (Exodus 32:4)

Notes and Personal Reflection:

_____

_____

_____

_____

_____

_____

_____

_____

_____

_____

_____

_____

_____

_____

_____

_____

CHAPTER 3

REQUIREMENTS AND

QUALIFICATIONS

The qualifications of leaders cannot be compromised. These qualifications are vital because God has a double standard when it comes to leadership (James 3:1). These qualifications will establish trust and influence with the members of your church. This is vital because a leader's influence must be greater than the people's resistance. If someone can trust you, it's likely that person will become your friend and be willing to work with you. If a person can get along with you, they will also follow you.

"This is a true saying, if a man desire the office of a bishop, he desireth a good work. A bishop then must be blameless, the husband of one wife, vigilant, sober, of good behaviour, given to hospitality, apt to teach; Not given to wine, no striker, not greedy of filthy lucre; but patient, not a brawler, not covetous; One that ruleth well his own house, having his children in subjection with all gravity; (For if a man know not how to rule his own house, how shall

he take care of the church of God?) Not a novice, lest being lifted up with pride he fall into the condemnation of the devil. Moreover he must have a good report of them which are without; lest he fall into reproach and the snare of the devil. Likewise must the deacons be grave, not doubletongued, not given to much wine, not greedy of filthy lucre; Holding the mystery of the faith in a pure conscience. And let these also first be proved; then let them use the office of a deacon, being found blameless. Even so must their wives be grave, not slanderers, sober, faithful in all things. Let the deacons be the husbands of one wife, ruling their children and their own houses well. For they that have used the office of a deacon well purchase to themselves a good degree, and great boldness in the faith which is in Christ Jesus" (I Timothy 3:1-13).

"Then the twelve summoned the multitude of the disciples and said, "It is not desirable that we should leave the word of God and serve tables. Therefore, brethren, seek out from among you seven men of good reputation, full of the Holy Spirit and wisdom, whom we may appoint over this business; but we will give ourselves continually to prayer and to the ministry of the word" (Acts 6:2-4).

"For this reason I left you in Crete, that you should set in order the things that are lacking, and appoint elders in every city as I commanded you— if a man is blameless, the husband of one wife, having faithful children not accused of dissipation or insubordination. For a bishop must be blameless, as a steward of God, not self-willed, not quick-tempered, not given to wine, not violent, not greedy for money, but hospitable, a lover of what is good, sober-minded, just, holy, self-controlled, holding fast the faithful word as he has been taught, that he may be able, by sound doctrine, both to exhort and convict those who contradict" (Titus 1:5-9).

Even in the Old Testament there has always been a different standard for leaders and laymen. God told Moses to select able men who he knew to be elders of the people and those who feared God, loved truth and hated covetousness. I believe those men were individuals that Moses had watched and observed for a period of time. They were proven and had the ability to operate in longevity, commitment, and obedience.

"Moreover thou shalt provide out of all the people able men, such as fear God, men of truth, hating covetousness; and place such over them, to be rulers of thousands, and

rulers of hundreds, rulers of fifties, and rulers of tens" (Exodus 18:21).

Elders & Deacons Have A Mantle To Serve

A deacon has the gift of the ministry of helps. A deacon must be joined to his or her senior leader and have a love for God's people.

Elders and deacons alike should avoid the mistake Aaron made! Aaron forgot who he was serving, and he tried to please the people by serving them, not Moses. Elders and deacons are to serve the senior leader and not try to please the people.

Elders and deacons should follow the patterns set by the apostles in the book of Acts. The apostles chose not to leave what God gave them to do but delegated the work to seven other men which could have been deacons to help meet the needs of the people.

The apostles understood that anything that would move them out of their purpose would cause them to miss what God had called them to do. The apostles refused to allow an urgent need to distract them or take them out of their God-ordained purpose.

The apostles chose seven men full of the Holy Ghost and wisdom whose primary responsibility was to wait on or serve the apostles and not just the widows at the tables. The deacon's primary responsibility was also to deal with any congregational problems that popped up and would take the apostles away from their calling! These deacons were joined to the apostles to serve them.

OWNERSHIP

God wants elders and deacons to occupy like it is theirs. A pastor will put a leader over something and they have to run it like it actually belongs to them, knowing it's another man's work. In Luke 19:11, the nobleman (Pastor) went to establish another ministry in another country, so he left some elders in charge by giving them some duties. Only two were able to get results; and one was lazy and did nothing, but he still wanted the position and the title of an elder. A leader will put his heart into the ministry if he is joined to the pastor.

In order to begin to operate under the principle of "ownership" a leader has to begin to give of himself or herself and of his or her substance. The leader has to care about the ministry and the vision; he or she has to think about it, pray for it, feel for it, and give up for it even though his or her name is not on the sign out front.

Not all leaders are given the same level of responsibility. All leaders do not have the same measure of anointing and they should be secure in their own measure. Leaders should be mature and not be jealous of another leader's measure or reward.

"And Moses chose able men out of all Israel and made them heads over the people; rulers of thousands, rulers of hundreds, rulers of fifties, an rulers of tens" (Exodus 18:25).

Elders in your church: (I Tim. 3:1-13; Acts 6:2-4; Titus 1:5-9; Ex. 18:21).

- ❖ must not give people a reason to criticize him;
- ❖ must have only one wife (or husband);
- ❖ must be self–controlled;
- ❖ must be wise;
- ❖ must be respected by others;
- ❖ must be ready to welcome guests (hospitable);

- ❖ must be able to teach;
- ❖ must not drink too much wine;
- ❖ must not like to fight;
- ❖ must be gentle and peaceable;

- ❖ must not love money;

- ❖ must be a good family leader, having children who cooperate with full respect (If someone does not know how to lead the family, how can that person take care of God's church?

- ❖ must not be a new believer;

- ❖ must also have the respect of people who are not in the church so he will not be criticized by others and caught in the devil's trap;

- ❖ must be an <u>example</u> and set the pattern (regularly attending Sunday school, bible class, all corporate settings such as meetings, prayer, etc.)

Deacons and deaconess in the church:

- ❖ must be respected by others; not saying things they do not mean;
- ❖ must not drink too much wine;
- ❖ must not try to get rich by cheating others;
- ❖ with a clear conscience they must follow the secret of the faith that God made known to us;
- ❖ must be tested and proven first;
- ❖ must be trustworthy in everything;
- ❖ must have only one wife (or husband);
- ❖ must be good leaders of their children and own families;
- ❖ must be an example and set the pattern (regularly attending Sunday school, bible class, all corporate settings such as meetings, prayer, etc.)

Notes and Personal Reflection:

_____

_____

_____

_____

_____

_____

_____

_____

_____

_____

_____

_____

_____

_____

Chapter 4

CHARACTERISTICS AND QUALITIES

There are many characteristics and qualities a leader should possess. In this section I will name a few.

A leader should be trustworthy, flexible, open, and humble. Leaders should be capable of bringing help to the vision of your church financially and spiritually. Leaders should have the ability to pour into others the vision that has been poured into them and have the ability to train and teach individuals how to stay on the God-given route until the assignment is finished. Leaders should have the ability to refresh, renew, strengthen, and encourage their pastor and others. (II Corinthians 7:6, 13; I Corinthians 4:17, Philippians 2:19-20).

Leaders should be able to master the office that they hold. To master something means to perfect, be highly skilled in it, able to operate in maturity, or bring to full usage. There are three steps that should be taken before coming into the office of an elder or deacon (Colossians. 3:9, 10, 12, 23; 4:6; Ephesians 4:22, 29: Philippians 3:20). First, you have to step into maturity. This involves your conversation and your conduct. The second step is to step into servant hood; serving out of devotion and not out of duty. Finally, you step into the gifts and callings of God.

You have to understand the difference between spiritual gifts given by the Holy Spirit and the ministry of the Church (I Corinthians 12:7-10, 28; Ephesians 4:11), and a mature Godly lifestyle (II Timothy 2:1-4). Examples of this would be having the gift of prophecy but not having the office of a prophet or prophetess or having the gift of healing but not the calling of a pastor.

Deacons walking worthy! It is essential that leaders have a prayer life that reflects Christ, a worship life that affects a worship service, and a word life that affects every area of life. Deacons have the ability to keep unity (Ephesians 4:3), and should always be thinking ministry and not self; knowing how to put out fires without gasoline. Deacons help end disputes, solve problems, relieve fears, remove assumptions, and provide financial support for the ministry. Deacons should work together toward one goal and understand how their gifts compliment one another.

> *Leaders must think 'ministry'*
> *and not 'self'.*

'MUST BE' Is A Demand And Not A Desire

"… if a man desire the office of a bishop, he desireth a good work. A bishop then must be…" (I Timothy 3:1-7)

Any office or position we hold demands certain qualifications and duties. If you release the office or position you can then release the qualifications and duties. What I've learned throughout my years of ministry is that most people want to hold onto the position and release the qualifications and duties.

Why would God give you an office or position without <u>demands</u>? Some people want to present their gifts and callings to God without repentance (Romans 11:29) but when there is no change, then will come a reproach against your ministry.

Spiritual Maturity

You can't equate *spiritual maturity* with *gifts, callings, or what you know spiritually or naturally.* Paul the apostle equated spiritual maturity with the absence of carnality in one's life-envy, strife, divisions (I Corinthians 3:3).

What you know can hurt you!

❖ We know more than we are doing;
❖ What you know doesn't qualify spiritual maturity;
❖ What you know can place you in a position that you can't handle;
❖ What you know **WITH APPLICATION** can prepare you for any test that God gives you;
❖ To know a little **WITH APPLICATION** is better than to know a lot with theory;
❖ Trial and error isn't the best teacher but it's someone who has experience in what you need to know and is willing to teach it to you.

Maturity (Meat Only)

What does it mean, **'meat only' (Hebrews 5:14)**? Every anointing has a different type of warfare and process. *It is vital that we understand the progression of the tests,*

temptations, and development of these anointings *(meat only).* Leaders that are under the leadership of 'a Jeremiah 3:15', a Jethro, a Deborah, or an apostle Paul understand the progression of a corporate vision and the continuity that flows from the senior leader to leadership as it relates to correction and direction. Those that are led by the Spirit of God are the sons of God (Romans 8:14).

The best way to learn is **BY EXPERIENCE**. A leader should not be a *NOVICE* (I Timothy 3:6). A novice is a beginner, one that begins something; an inexperienced person. Timothy was not a novice but he was a well experienced senior leader with a proven track record (Philippians 2:19-24; II Timothy 2:1-3) The centurion officer was not a novice but had experience in delegated authority. *'but said to Jesus, speak the word and my servant will be healed'* (Matthew 8:8-9) Godly experience will increase your faith.

Notes and Personal Reflection:

_____

_____

_____

_____

_____

_____

_____

_____

_____

_____

_____

_____

_____

_____

_____

Chapter 5

THE VOICE OF GOD

"And when He brings out His own sheep, He goes before them; and the sheep follow Him, for they know His voice" (John 10:4).

Why is it so crucial that leaders know and obey the voice of God? **God will primarily speak to the senior pastor He has placed over a local church, relaying the plans, instructions, assignment, directions and thoughts concerning that ministry to him or her. As the leader of that ministry he or she must know what God is saying to that local body He has placed them over.** In addition, leaders that work under the senior leader in any leadership capacity (prison ministry, nursery, Sunday school, etc.) should be able to recognize what the Lord is saying about the ministry that they are over or a part of. They should have the ability to know what God is saying to their specific area of ministry and connect it to what God has already said to the senior leader as it relates to the overall vision of that ministry. **What God is saying to the senior leader down to those under him or her should be in alignment with what God is speaking or has already said to that local body**.

Seven times in the book of revelation God compels us to hear and listen to what the Spirit is saying to the churches;

"He who has an ear, let him hear what the Spirit says to the churches" (Revelation 2:7, 11, 17, 29; 3:6, 13, 22).

The fact that it is mentioned seven times within these two chapters of the book of Revelation in essence show us how important God feels it is that we know and hear His voice.

We must know God's voice because His voice is His word (Deuteronomy 28:1-14). As believers, and especially as leaders, it is important that we are able to recognize God's voice through His written word, the rhema word, prophecy, dreams, visions, divine encounters with nature or everyday living, and through His Spirit and our spirits. This is to ensure that we are able to receive and apply the wisdom and revelation God wants to give us in order to live out our God given purpose and destiny.

The key to hearing God is the Holy Spirit. *Then the Spirit of the Lord will come upon you, and you will prophesy* (I Samuel 10:6). *The Spirit of God came upon the messengers of Saul, and they also prophesied* (I Samuel 19:20). *And it happened, when the Spirit rested upon them, that they prophesied* (Numbers 11:25).

God's voice brings life and order (Genesis 1:2). The Holy Spirit hovering connotes *"sweeping or moving.* "God said" occurs ten times in chapter one of Genesis. If you are hearing God's voice on a consistent basis, your life will have order and life. Something will die, that is trying to stop you from living and something will leave that is causing disorder. God's voice is a creative force.

God wants to create and develop a track record of Him leading us by His voice-the spirit of revelation (Deuteronomy 28:1; Jeremiah 33:3; Isaiah 50:4; John 16:13-15). Wisdom and humility is where revelation breaks through (Proverbs 9:1, 16:19; Ephesians 1:17). Wisdom builds the house, humility keeps the house standing, and revelation keeps the house moving forward in God. The Spirit of revelation will bring you into a place, situation, or season of *"such a time as this"* (Esther 4:14). To whatever degree we move in revelation (present truth) will determine whether or not we win the war. You can build something fairly successful with wisdom but you won't win any war without revelation (Ephesians 1:17).

Wisdom is truth we've learned and experienced about God, ourselves and satan and we have no doubt about it. Revelation is the strategy, instruction, and plan that we need in any given situation we are in or find ourselves in. Revelation and wisdom work most effectively when teamed up together to yield the best results: revelation produces present truth, which keeps us progressing and makes the wisdom we've already gained relevant to whatever the situation or circumstance we encounter.

Ephesians 1:17- wisdom and revelation
Proverbs 4:7- wisdom is the principle thing

Then God said, "Let there be light"; and there was light (Genesis 1:3).

Jesus says that His sheep know His voice. If you obey the voice of God it will keep you on top. Why should God speak to us if we are not willing to obey? If we don't sincerely want to do God's will we won't have the capacity to listen to His voice. **As leaders we must discipline ourselves to walk in obedience to what we already know is the will of God.**

"Now it shall come to pass if you diligently obey the voice of Lord your God, to observe carefully all His commandments which I command you today, that the Lord your God will set you above all nations of the earth. And all these blessings shall come upon you

and overtake you, because you obey the voice of the Lord your God" (Deuteronomy 28:1- 2).

What is God's Word? The word of God is the mind, the will, and the knowledge of God. It is active and alive. The word of God is God. (Hebrews 4:12)

Throughout the old and new testaments God spoke to man through dreams and visions. What is a dream or vision? **(Numbers 12:6; Job 33:14-16).** A dream or vision is a release of revelation, whether natural or spiritual, that comes at a time when your body is at peace and you are settled. As an effective way to bypass the walls of defense and pride that we sometimes have within our hearts and souls, there are several reasons why the Lord uses dreams and visions as a means of communicating to individuals:

❖ To open our ears and get our attention or warn us;
❖ To bring destruction;
❖ To show struggles we have within ourselves;

❖ To help us be aware of things taking place in our daily lives by guiding, directing, or instructing us;

❖ To communicate what's in His heart

85% of the dreams God gives you will be about you. Godly dreams will always be a means to causing us to have a closer, deeper relationship with Him and will be consistent to the nature, character, and teaching of the Lord. Dreams however can be of a soulish and even demonic source. The great thing is that having a healthy prayer life along with developing the gift of discernment on a greater level will help you to interpret the dreams you receive with the proper interpretation and meaning accurately and know the source of your dreams.

What is Prophecy? Prophecy is speaking the mind and heart of God as revealed by the Holy Spirit. True prophecy is the voice of God. Revelation 19:10 says that, 'the testimony of Jesus is the spirit of prophecy'. It releases the power of God and activates God's authority in our lives.

To prophesy is one of the Godly operations we should pursue (I Corinthians 14:1).

> *"Then the Spirit of the Lord will come upon you, and you will prophesy." (I Samuel 10:6).*

> *"The Spirit of God came upon the messengers of Saul, and they also prophesied" (I Samuel 19:20).*

> *"And it happened, when the Spirit rested upon them, that they prophesied" (Numbers 11:25).*

Is it safe to be led by a prophecy or dream? Here are four questions that can be a guideline in knowing whether or not you can be led by a prophecy or dream:

1. What is the source or origin of the Prophecy or dream (I Samuel 3:1-20; Job 33:14-18)? If the answer is God then the nature of the prophecy or dream will be based on His love.

2. Does the prophecy or dream agree with your spirit? If it does then it will align with other words or dreams or warnings you have received from God (Jeremiah 23:23-24).

3. Does the prophecy or dream have anything to do with your destiny or identity? If so, is the timing of the word or dream correct? Is the amount of the word given correct? The timing of a word and how much should be released is critical in any prophecy or revelatory release (Acts 21:10-14).

4. If other prophets or prophetic people are present, do they bear witness with the word or dream that was released? (Acts 11:28-29; I Corinthians 14:32-33).

The Apostle Paul told Timothy to war with the prophecies previously spoken over his life (I Timothy 1:18). *A point to note:* The Apostle said 'prophecies'-more than one. Confirmation and testing is always in order. The Apostle Paul told the Thessalonica church not to despise prophecies but to test them and set their course by the prophecies (I Thessalonians 5:20-21).

In whatever form God's voice may come, it comes to bring life and order (Genesis 1:2). His voice is a creative force. If you are hearing God's voice on a consistent basis, your life will have order and life. Knowing the voice of God will help you to have a clear understanding of His will for your life (Acts 9:6,15).

As a leader, different situations will arise that will call for different types of revelation or strategies from God. During these times you must seek God for His thoughts or plans. The key to hearing God is the Holy Spirit. You must also have 'an ear to hear':

"He awakens Me morning by morning, He awakens my ear to hear as the learned" (Isaiah 50:4c).

> Leaders can't lead without the voice of God.

Notes and Personal Reflection:

_____

_____

_____

_____

_____

_____

_____

_____

_____

_____

_____

_____

_____

_____

_____

Chapter 6

INNER HEALING AND BREAKING INNER VOWS

One major hindrance that causes individuals to not move forward spiritually in their walk with God and in their relationship with others is the need for inner healing. We need to be healed inwardly because of life experiences, situations, or circumstances that have caused emotional pain in our heart, soul, and spirits.

Many believers, even leaders, are unknowingly operating in ministry on a regular basis but because of the need for inner healing are having problems with trust and won't submit to the leadership God has placed in their lives as a protective spiritual covering (the senior leader or pastor), or with other leaders or believers, working under delegated authority, knowing how to interact with individuals that may be working under them, etc. all because of inner hurts and pain that they refuse to deal with or are

afraid to deal with, not realizing the lid that this hindrance is placing upon their destiny in God.

Jesus stated that He was anointed to do five things. All of those five things dealt with the ministry of deliverance in one aspect or another:

> *"The Spirit of the LORD is upon Me, Because He has anointed Me To preach the gospel to the poor; He has sent Me to heal the brokenhearted, to proclaim liberty to the captives and recovery of sight to the blind, to set at liberty those who are oppressed" (Luke 4:18).*

We want to focus on Jesus being the healer of the brokenhearted which allows us to be healed inwardly. He came to bring healing when our hearts have been broken into pieces, wounded, and hurt. When this happens to us we oftentimes make what is called an 'inner vow'

An inner vow is a promise we make to ourselves. It is a type of stronghold that deals with the need for inner healing that is often hidden deep within us that is used to protect our heart from pain and hurts without the power of the cross. The word 'stronghold' can be found in the word of God, which is a false idea in your mind, something you accept to be true without proving it to be so. **A stronghold in your thoughts is designed to prevent you from recognizing and dealing with hurts, pain, and sin.**

"For the weapons of our warfare are not carnal but mighty in God for pulling down strongholds casting down arguments and every high thing that exalts itself against the knowledge of God, bringing every thought into captivity to the obedience of Christ, and being ready to punish all disobedience when your obedience is fulfilled" (II Corinthians 10:4-6).

The inner vow starts with thoughts in the head we tell ourselves but grows within the heart. Most inner vows are not spoken but are revealed in our actions. Many inner vows are made in our childhood or early years and are oftentimes forgotten in the head, but not in the heart.

Some examples of inner vows people make are:

> *'I will never trust anyone anymore.'*
> *'I will never let anyone hurt me again.'*
> *'No one will ever walk over me.'*
> *'I don't ever want to get married.'*
> *'I'll never get married again.'*
> *'I'll never get close to anyone.'*
> *'I'm not going to take that.'*
> *'Don't feel sorry for me.'*
> *'Yes, it hurt me but I'm not worried about that.'*
> *'I will always be gentle with others.'*
> *'I will always see the best in people.'*
> *'I'm just going to go to work and do my job and not fool with these people.'*

Although inner vows are made with the intent to protect oneself, the fact of the matter is they don't work. In fact, if we begin to allow God to show us the root cause of the inner vows we've made, we will find that behind every inner vow is a lie and behind that lie is some type of fear that we had or have.

The key for us is to allow God, through the power of prayer, to show us the inner vows we have made so that we can begin to release the hurts so He can begin to heal the wounds that are within us.

Genesis chapter 32 talks about how Jacob was wrestling with who he had become, although he was really Israel. He was not born to be a slickster, trying to get over on people- I believe that is who he became because of some inner vows he'd made or the need for inner healing within his heart and soul. He probably made some inner vows like this, 'Well, this is just how I am and I'll always be like this. I'll always be getting over on people before they get over on me.' Then in verse 22 the scripture goes on to tell us how Jacob wrestled with a man (God) who asked Jacob what his name was. The man challenged Jacob telling him, 'no that's who you became- break those vows' (paraphrased). I believe that unless a leader realizes that the enemy was trying to mold and shape them into becoming someone they were really not before they gave their life to Christ, that their leadership ability, once they become a part of the Body of Christ, will be affected unless they break the inner vows they've made. It will affect their ability to impart into those they are leading, or only at best, allow them to give out of their intellect as opposed to real true personal experience because of their own relationship with God. Inner vows that haven't been broken can affect a leader's ability to judge and discern. These are two essential attributes every leader needs to have if they want to be able to lead effectively. Without inner healing taking place or inner vows being broken in their own lives, their ability to lead will be restricted.

How to get rid of inner vows:

1. Recognize the inner vow(s) that you have made.

2. Forgive the individual(s) who played any part in causing you to make the inner vow.

3. Confess and repent for making the inner vow(s).

4. Ask God to pull down the stronghold of the inner vow and then revoke its power over you.

It is imperative that leaders break inner vows and receive inner healing because the enemy wants to use these things to set you up for failure or a fall as you go along in ministry. One of the greatest tools the enemy uses against believers is the spirit of deception. He wants you to think you are okay because of the position you hold and the success you are experiencing in ministry. It will only be a matter of time before satan begins to attack you in the areas you haven't dealt with in your life that can, in the long run, prove to be detrimental to you personally and to your ministry.

> **Inner vows don't work. We must use the right weapons.**

Notes and Personal Reflection:

_____

_____

_____

_____

_____

_____

_____

_____

_____

_____

_____

_____

_____

_____

CHAPTER 7

UNDERSTANDING YOUR CALLING, ANOINTING, AND SPIRITUAL GIFTS

I want to start this chapter by explaining what understanding is. Understanding is the knowledge and ability to judge. To understand is to grasp the meaning of and to comprehend. Godly understanding will reinforce what you know about God, yourself, your gifts and callings and the ministry you are in and more. Understanding will establish what you know and make it firm, stable, solid, and sound.

When the scripture said lean not to your own understanding but acknowledge Him and He will direct your path in Proverbs 3:5, God is not telling us that we don't need understanding but He is telling us to walk by faith and not by understanding. In I Chronicles 12:32 when the scripture states that the sons of Isssachar had understanding of the timing of God that word 'understanding' is the Hebrew word 'Biyn', which is 'prophetic understanding' which has the implications of hearing God's voice in detail and knowing what, how, and when to do something.

"And of the children of Issachar, which were men that had understanding of the times, to know what Israel ought to do; the heads of them were two hundred; and all their brethren were at their commandment" (I Chronicles 12:32).

"Get skillful and Godly wisdom, get understanding (discernment, comprehension, and interpretation); do not forget and do not turn back from the words of my mouth. Forsake not [Wisdom], and she will keep, defend, and protect you; love her, and she will guard you. The beginning of wisdom is: get wisdom (skillful and Godly wisdom)! [For skillful and Godly wisdom is the principal thing.] And with all you have gotten, get understanding (discernment, comprehension, and interpretation)" (Proverbs 4:5-7).

"It is as sport to [self–confident] fool to do wickedness, but to have skillful and Godly wisdom is pleasure and relaxation to a man of understanding" (Proverbs 10:23).

"He who is slow to anger has great understanding, but he who is hasty of spirit exposes and exalts his folly" (Proverbs 14:29).

"Through skillful and Godly wisdom is a house (a life, a home, a family) built, and by understanding it is established [on a sound and good foundation], and by knowledge shall its chambers [of every area] be filled with all precious and pleasant riches" (Proverbs 24:3-4).

UNDERSTANDING YOUR CALL

"Therefore, my brothers, be all the more eager to make your calling and election sure. For if you do these things, you will never fall" (II Peter 1:10).

What does it mean to be 'called'? The word 'call' in the Greek means "to incite by word", "to provoke to action". Webster defines the word 'call' as "to make a request or demand", to summon". A call always comes with specific instructions- what to do, how to do, where to go, to whom to go to, how to act, what to say, and to whom to say it to! The call will come with instructions that you will need revelation from God to carry out.

"After these things the LORD appointed other seventy also, and sent them two and two before his face into every city and place, whither he himself would come. Therefore said he unto them, The harvest truly is great, but the labourers are few: pray ye therefore the Lord of the harvest, that he would send forth labourers into his harvest. Go your ways: behold, I send you forth as lambs among wolves. Carry neither purse, nor scrip, nor shoes: and salute no man by the way. And into whatsoever house ye enter, first say, Peace be to this house. And if the son of peace be there, your peace shall rest upon it: if not, it shall turn to you again. And in the same house remain, eating and drinking such things as they give: for the labourer is worthy of his hire. Go not from house to house. And into whatsoever city ye enter, and they receive you, eat such things as are set before you: And heal the sick that are therein, and say unto them, The kingdom of God is come nigh unto you. But into whatsoever city ye enter, and they receive you not, go your ways out into the streets of the same, and say Even the very dust of your city, which cleaveth on us, we do wipe off against you: notwithstanding be ye sure of this, that the kingdom of God is come nigh unto you." (Luke 10:1-11)

Responding to the "Call" causes you to experience a divine encounter with God! Moses (Exodus 3:1-10); Elisha (I Kings 19:19-21); Amos (Amos 7:14-15); Paul (Acts 9:1-19;13:1,2).

A call comes with an anointing to fulfill what God has called you to do. (II Peter 1:3, 4) Fulfilling a call comes with what I call the two "T"s- Training and Timing. Training is when you are being mentored and receiving instructions. This means you're in a place of being subject to another for direction and correction. Timing is a specific time and not just any time!

There are characteristics of a "Call":

Discipline – Training to ensure proper behavior. It is the practice or methods of teaching and enforcing acceptable patterns of behavior (II Peter 1:5-9; I Corinthians 9:24-27).

Vision – A plan; someone with unusual foresight; they are able to think ahead; they have the ability to see possible future problems and obstacles (Proverbs 29:18).

Energy – the ability or power to work or make an effort; liveliness and forcefulness (John 4:31-34).

Motivation (zeal) – a feeling of enthusiasm, interest, or commitment that makes somebody want to do something; energetic and unflagging enthusiasm, especially for a cause or idea (Philippians 3:14).

Confidence – self assurance or a belief in your ability to succeed (Philippians 1:6).

UNDERSTANDING YOUR ANOINTING

"The Spirit of the LORD is upon Me, because He has anointed Me to preach the gospel to the poor; He has sent Me to heal the brokenhearted, to proclaim liberty to the captives, and recovery of sight to the blind, to set at liberty those who are oppressed" (Luke 4:18).

Every believer is anointed by God. *"Now He who establishes us with you in Christ and has anointed us is God...." (II Corinthians 1:21)*

What is the anointing? Apostle Otis Lockett defines it in this way: The anointing is my God-given right and ability to do what I do with the full backing of God. My wife says the anointing of God is a deposit He places in our heart and this is our guarantee. The anointing of God always brings great results. (Daniel 1:9,15; Ruth 3:3-11; Judges 14:6; I Corinthians 5:3).

When it comes to the anointing we must ask ourselves these questions: Am I doing what God wants me to do? Do I have the right to do what I am doing? Is God backing what I 'm doing and what is the evidence?

David defeated Goliath because he was anointed to do what he did to Goliath (I Samuel 16:13). The anointing is designed to fight. It is designed to annihilate, destroy, defeat, and punish the enemy. The text stated that from that day forward the Spirit of the Lord was upon David. The anointing did not leave David. When we are anointed we are not lacking in anointing but we may be lacking in the areas of character or obedience.

We can do the work of God and not do the will of God. God wants us to do His will. *"Not everyone who says to Me, 'Lord, Lord,' shall enter the kingdom of heaven, but he who does the will of My Father in heaven. Many will say to Me in that day, 'Lord, Lord, have we not prophesied in Your name, cast out demons in*

Your name, and done many wonders in Your name?' And then I will declare to them, 'I never knew you; depart from Me, you who practice lawlessness!" (Matthew 7:21-23)

The anointing has to be activated. To activate is 'to start something working as designed by its maker'. What activates the anointing? Faith, prayer and perseverance activates the anointing. You have to believe that you are anointed (Matthew 13:58). You have to pray daily for what you are doing (James 5:16) and you have to persevere where the greatest pressure is and take a step in that direction (Romans 5:3-4).

There are certain signs and functions of the anointing (Mark 16:17-18). Some of the signs and functions of the anointing are to eliminate obstacles and solve problems. The anointing will give you the ability to communicate with others; it give us the ability to handle demonic situations in our family, job, church and more. The anointing enables us to overcome false pretenses and help others. The anointing will resolve family problems. It will cause finances to increase in our life and bring divine healing into our life. It will give us the influence and authority God wants us to have within a town, city, or nation.

The anointing will work in our lives in three major ways. It will not only come upon us but it will work within us. The anointing came upon Jesus and He heard a voice from His Father saying, "This is my beloved son in whom I am well pleased.' The anointing works on the inward part of us so that we will know that God loves us. This kind of love and anointing gives us the inner healing that we need. It goes to the root (Matthew 3:16-17).

The anointing on the inside along with inner healing helps us to get things done in a much better way. The anointing on the outside, praying for others, laying hands, casting out demons and laboring with leaders and laymen will help the Body of Christ in a greater way. The anointing on your life will be tested and tempted (Matthew 4:11). It will help you to walk in your destiny and your identity (Luke 4:16).

There are three proof–text scriptures that help us to understand the anointing on our lives:

"Then answered Jesus and said unto them, Verily, verily, I say unto you, The Son can do

nothing of himself, but what he seeth the Father do: for what things soever he doeth, these also doeth the Son likewise." (John 5:19)

"Then Samuel took the horn of oil, and anointed him in the midst of his brethren: and the Spirit of the LORD came upon David from that day forward. So Samuel rose up, and went to Ramah." (I Samuel 16:13)

"The Spirit of the Lord is upon me, because he hath anointed me to preach the gospel to the poor; he hath sent me to heal the brokenhearted, to preach deliverance to the captives, and recovering of sight to the blind, to set at liberty them that are bruised." (Luke 4:18)

UNDERSTANDING YOUR SPIRITUAL GIFTS

My Gift Will Help Me Be What I Was Called To Be

Do I know my spiritual gift(s)? Do I know what I was called to be, purposed to be, or born to be? As believers we can trace our destiny – what we were purposed or called to be and do – back to Genesis 1:26-28 and our identity can be traced back to Genesis 2:7. The devil and memories of our crucified flesh desire our destiny and identity to be traced back to Genesis 3:9-10.

The Holy Spirit's power will reveal to us what our gifting is and what we are called to be and what our assignment is today.

In his book, Your Spiritual Gifts Can Help Your Church Grow, C. Peter Wagner gives us a definitive description of spiritual gifts versus natural talents and abilities: What is a spiritual gift? It is a special attribute given by the Holy Spirit to every member of the Body of Christ according to God's grace for use within the context of the Body. How many spiritual gifts are there? What do we mean when we say 'special'? *Something that is uncommon, noteworthy, or unique.* What is an 'attribute'? *An inherent characteristic or quality.*

The great majority of the spiritual gifts mentioned in the bible are found in three key chapters:

Romans 12:6-8; these are the gifts of prophecy, service, teaching, exhortation, giving, leadership and mercy.

I Corinthians 12:8-10 and 28; these are word of wisdom, word of knowledge, faith, healing, miracles, discerning of spirits, tongues, interpretation of tongues, Apostle, helps and administration.

Ephesians 4:11; the gifts are Evangelist, Pastor and Prophet.

Other chapters that include important details concerning spiritual gifts are I Corinthians 7, I Corinthians 13 and 14, Ephesians 3 and I Peter 4; gifts of celibacy, hospitality, voluntary poverty, intercession, martyrdom, deliverance, missionary, and worship leader.

Different 'gifts' are the special abilities given by the Holy Spirit according to God's grace. Different 'ministries' are the work, assignment, or call. Different 'activities' are the scope or range of the call or assignment. (I Corinthians 12:4-6). Don't confuse spiritual gifts with natural talents, a Christian role, or fruits of the Spirit. Your gift will make room for you and help your ministry to advance. Your gift will always fit into the ministry God has placed you in. If you experiment with a gift and consistently find that what it is supposed to do does not happen, you probably have discovered another one of the gifts God has not given you.

What is the difference between a natural talent and a spiritual gift? A *natural talent is an ability that we have that makes up our personality and personal identity as a human being that is not necessarily tied into being a believer, but a spiritual gift is exclusively for the believer.*

Each one of us can do a spiritual profile on our gifts, callings and assignment. To create your personal profile ask yourself the following questions:

A. What is my gift(s)?
B. What is the fruit of my gift(s)?
C. How did I discover my gift(s)?
D. What was I called or born to be?
E. What is my assignment?
F. How is my assignment affecting the ministry?

Will my assignment change or will it be built upon? When will it be completed?

The *gift* is given from God and the *office* is given by the Church (I Corinthians 12:7,11,18; Acts 13:2,14:14-15; Titus 1:5; Galatians 2:9).

See the spiritual gifts charts on the next page that God gave me for my own leadership team several years ago to gain insight on the gifts, callings, and anointing that your own leaders have, and how they can work together to further the vision of your ministry.

Coming Out Of The Old Into The New

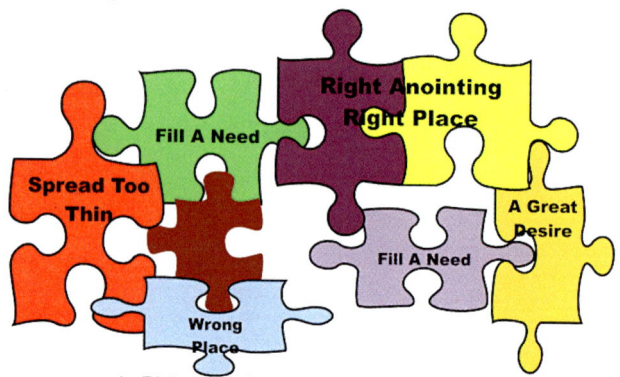

1. Right Anointing + Right Place = Great Results
2. Spread Too Thin You Won't Win (You Will Burn Out)
3. Right Anointing + Wrong Place = Less Results

How To Build

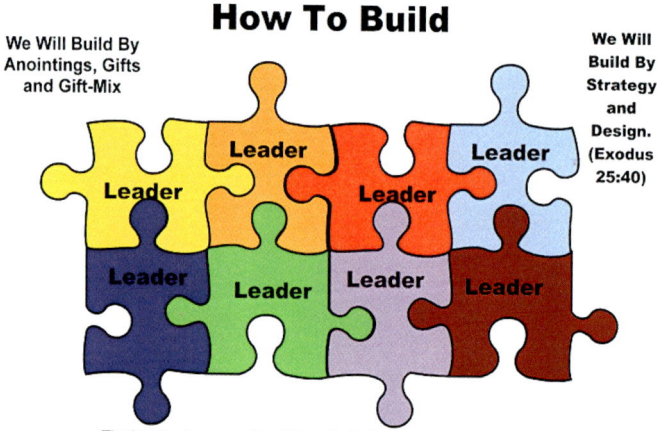

The burden is removed and the yoke is destroyed because of the anointing.
Isa. 10:27 (paraphrased).

The Body will be working together because each part is working in its proper place,
causing growth and strength in love. Eph 4:16 (paraphrased).

Notes and Personal Reflection:

_____

_____

_____

_____

_____

_____

_____

_____

_____

_____

_____

_____

_____

_____

_____

Chapter 8
SPIRITUAL WARFARE

Are demons for today? Yes! God is sovereign but satan is active.

What is spiritual warfare? **It is the *spiritual confrontation between the kingdom of God and the kingdom of darkness*** *(Matthew 12:26-30; John 10:10; James 3:13-18; I Corinthians 2:12).* Spiritual warfare is real. We do not wrestle against flesh and blood, but we do wrestle against satan's kingdom.

"For we do not wrestle against flesh and blood, but against principalities, against powers, against the rulers of the darkness of this age, against spiritual hosts of wickedness in the heavenly places" (Ephesians 6:12).

What are demons? They are fallen angels and disembodied spirits (Isaiah 14:12-15; Revelation 12:3-9). Demons like to attack individuals, attach themselves to individuals, and infest the soul and body (Luke. 10:19; 13:16; Matthew 8:16).

Names we refer to the devil are, 'the wicked one', 'the god of this age', 'the prince of the air', 'Lucifer'. The goal of satan is to kill, steal and destroy (John 10:10). He wants to kill (stop) every move of God and to hinder the Kingdom of God and believers from carrying out every assignment God has given the body of Christ to fulfill here on the earth. He wants to steal everything that God has blessed us with and given us dominion over. He desires to destroy everything that God has established for His glory. The two kingdoms are competing for the souls of every individual who inhabits the earth. The result is an ongoing battle between the visible realm and the invisible realm.

Just as God uses plans and strategies to carry out His plans so does the enemy. He uses them against believers to stop them from carrying out the Heavenly Father's goals. His most frequently and successfully used weapons is the spirit of deception. The devil loves to lie (Genesis 3:4) and he likes to deceive our minds with lies (Galatians 3:1).

"You are of your father the devil, and the desires of your father you want to do. He was a murderer from the beginning, and does not stand in the truth, because there is no truth in him. When he speaks a lie, he speaks from his own resources, for he is a liar and the father of it" (John 8:44).

"Whose minds the god of this age has blinded, who do not believe, lest the light of the gospel of the glory of Christ, who is the image of God, should shine on them" (II Corinthians 4:4).

"He has blinded their eyes and hardened their hearts, lest they should see with their eyes...." *(John 12:40a).*

Satan also likes to use the spirits of rejection and fear against believers. (Judges 6:12-15; Genesis 29:30-32; I John 4:18; Psalm 34:4; I Timothy 1:7)

There are 3 levels of spiritual warfare:
1. **Level one -** deals with casting out demons, deliverance from demonic oppression and possession.

2. **Level two** - deals with demonic influence relating to organizations such as cults, masons, eastern stars, elks, shriners, fraternities, and sororities, etc.

3. **Level three** - deals with demonic activity and influences that are principalities over geographical areas and regions of cities, towns, states, countries, and nations, etc.

As believers we have power over the devil! *(Mark 16:17; I John 3:8; Colossians 2:15).*

"I have given you the power to trample on snakes and scorpions and to defeat the power of your enemy satan" (Luke 10:19).

God has given us strategies against the enemy:

We must pray and ask God to help us hate the devil and his darkness.
"Do I not hate them, O Lord, who hate you? And do I not loathe those who rise up against you? I hate them with perfect hatred; I count them my enemies" (Psalm. 139:21-22).

We must desire to crush satan's head and his ways (Romans 16:20). We must destroy satan's communication system (II Corinthians 2:11, 10:5). We must develop a spiritual vocabulary as it relates to the devil (**ex. 'I bind you', 'I loose you', 'the blood is against you', 'I break your stronghold', 'I know your name')**. You must know the power of your words-when your words are anointed (Matthew 8:16).

We must pursue righteousness and hate darkness. (II Timothy 2:22) We must never give the devil any place through unforgiveness and unconfessed sin (Ephesians 4:26-27).

We can drive demons out and pull down strongholds. In order to pull down strongholds we must be able to receive from the Holy Spirit. We must do these three things:
1. Start with the natural;
2. Operate in faith;
3. The end result will be that you will finish in the supernatural. (Judges 6:14-16).

How to drive demons out:

You don't have to let a demon manifest before casting it out (Luke 4:41; Acts 5:16, 16:18). You don't have to talk to demons or ask their name before casting them out (Matthew 17:18). We can crowd demons out (Psalm 119:11; Acts 6:3). Demons can be starved out. They feed on the works of the flesh (Matthew 4:11). We can command demons to come out (Mark 6:17).

We must learn how to defend our territory. We must shut the door of evil because we have the power and authority to do so (Genesis 18:20-22; Ezekiel 22:30; Isaiah 22:22; Acts16:20).

As a leader you may think, why so much revelation on spiritual warfare? The reason is because warfare is a part of our lifestyle. A leader must understand that their call, anointing, and assignment all correlate with the type of warfare they will encounter. Without knowing this key factor, that individual will not understand what's taking place in their life if they are not aware of the connection. Not only will that leader experience warfare, but their spouses, children, and those working close to that person will also experience a certain amount of warfare because of their relationship to that leader. For example, from the beginning of their process, a pastor needs to be aware of the fact that they are called to be a pastor and will encounter the type of warfare that comes with the call, anointing, and assignment of a pastor. Their spouse and children will also encounter some attacks from the enemy. If we intend to transform cities and nations we must know our enemy. You will find a war zone chart at the end of this chapter that God gave me several years ago. This war zone chart displays revelation helpful to leaders that work closely to the senior leaders and the different levels of warfare they will encounter and the responsibility they have to perform.

The Inner Circle Level of Warfare & Responsibility

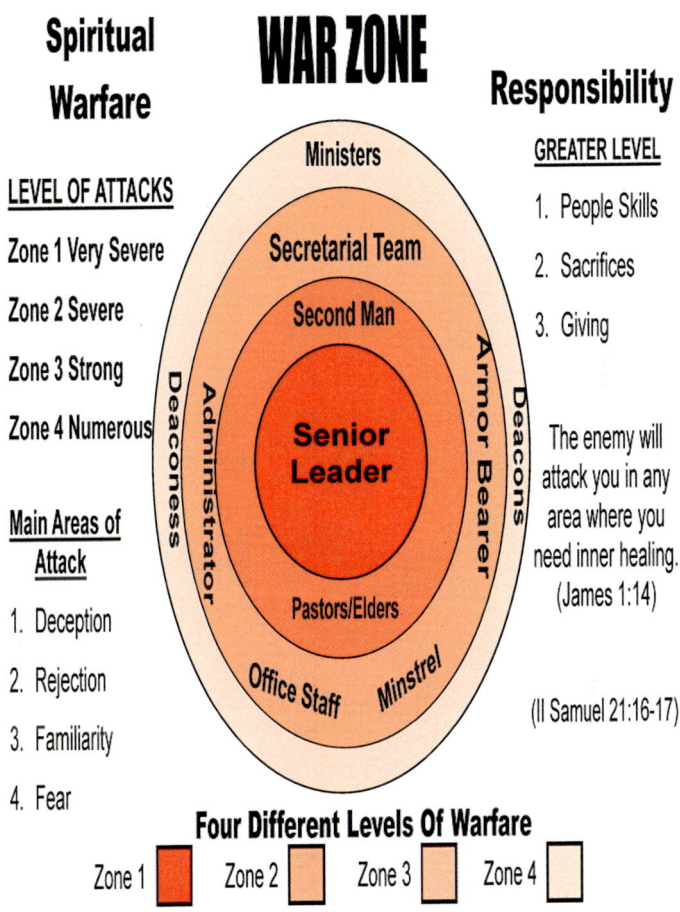

Spiritual Warfare

WAR ZONE

Responsibility

LEVEL OF ATTACKS

Zone 1 Very Severe

Zone 2 Severe

Zone 3 Strong

Zone 4 Numerous

Main Areas of Attack

1. Deception
2. Rejection
3. Familiarity
4. Fear

GREATER LEVEL

1. People Skills
2. Sacrifices
3. Giving

The enemy will attack you in any area where you need inner healing. (James 1:14)

(II Samuel 21:16-17)

Within the diagram:

Ministers

Secretarial Team

Second Man

Senior Leader

Pastors/Elders

Office Staff

Minstrel

Deaconess

Administrator

Armor Bearer

Deacons

Four Different Levels Of Warfare

Zone 1   Zone 2   Zone 3   Zone 4

Notes and Personal Reflection:

_____

_____

_____

_____

_____

_____

_____

_____

_____

_____

_____

_____

_____

_____

Chapter 9

UNDERSTANDING GOD'S AUTHORITY AND DELEGATED AUTHORITY

It is important that senior pastors and all the leaders in that ministry be joined to one another. Senior pastors provide spiritual covering to leaders within their ministry. A spiritual covering is a mantle of God's protection and presence over an individual's life because they have submitted themselves to God's chain of command and authority.

God's authority is His sovereign rule through the chain of command He has set in place on the earth and within the Body of Christ in order to carry out His purposes and plans, and to provide spiritual covering to those within His kingdom. God uses man and woman to carry out His desires here on earth and does so through delegated authority.

Delegated authority- _a portion of authority given to you by someone else. This type of authority is measured out and given based on the position and responsibility we have and it authorizes us to carry out certain functions. It also makes us a representative of that individual that gave us the authority. By accepting this authority we are also held accountable to carry out the responsibilities and functions designated to us._

One can only receive authority if they submit to authority (Matthew 3:15) and only to the degree of authority that we submit to is the degree of authority that we can operate in as we can see in the statement made by the centurion in Matthew 8:9:

"For I also am a man under authority, having soldiers under me. And I say to this one, 'Go,' and he goes; and to another, 'Come,' and he comes; and to my servant, 'Do this,' and he does it."

By the same token, when an individual **rejects authority** he reflects the fact that he has no authority over himself (Proverbs 25:28). The byproduct of anyone that attempts to operate in authority without being **under** authority is the spirit of rebellion. It is important that leaders working under the senior leader understand how to operate in that authority by carrying out every assignment they've been given to do. One of the main goals of any leader working under their senior pastor is to lighten his or her load.

> **God made a decision to use man and woman.**

Joshua was able to send out two spies into the land of Jericho (Joshua 2:1). They were able to carry out the assignment and bring back the information to their leader (Joshua 2:23).

The Apostle Paul was able to send Timothy to the Philippians because Paul was confident in his ability to carry out each assignment he gave to Timothy.

"For I have no one like-minded, who will sincerely care for your state. ......But you know his proven character, that as a son with

his father he served with me in the gospel. Therefore I hope to send him at once, as soon as I see how it goes with me. But I trust in the Lord that I myself shall also come shortly" *(Philippians 2:19-20, 22-23).*

In the local church God has delegated a full measure of authority to the senior pastor. Other leaders have a measure or a portion of the authority the senior leader has based upon their spiritual responsibility and positions within that local church.

We can see a great example of delegated authority of senior pastors and leaders that have been delegated authority under them as we look at Moses, Jethro, and the children of Israel.

"So when Moses' father-in-law saw all that he did for the people, he said, "What is this thing that you are doing for the people? Why do you alone sit, and all the people stand before you from morning until evening…...So Moses' father-in-law said to him, "The thing that you do is not good. Both you and these people who are with you will surely wear yourselves

out. For this thing is too much for you; you are not able to perform it by yourself. Listen now to my voice; I will give you counsel, and God will be with you: Stand before God for the people, so that you may bring the difficulties to God. And you shall teach them the statutes and the laws, and show them the way in which they must walk and the work they must do" *(Exodus 18:14, 17-20).*

Moses was the senior pastor. He was the one God had set over the children of Israel to lead them out of Egypt. He was the one who God gave the plans and instructions to and then passed them along to the children of Israel. God had Moses' father-in-law Jethro teach Moses about delegated authority.

As the senior leader, one of the main principles that he or she must understand and incorporate into their leadership operation is the ability to delegate the authority that God has given to them. This is so that he or she will not ***burn out*** and it is also so that that senior leader will have a ***successor*** who understands the vision of that ministry that is already prepared to take over the responsibilities of the senior leader or any major functions if the need arises. By training others and delegating authority to them, the senior leader is allowing their gifts and callings to be developed which is necessary in order to carry out the work and vision of that ministry.

Moses is a good example in the scripture of a leader who shows us how to delegate authority and appoint a successor.

"So Moses' father-in-law said to him, "The thing that you do is not good. Both you and these people who are with you will surely wear yourselves out. For this thing is too much for you; you are not able to perform it by yourself.......So Moses heeded the voice of his father-in-law and did all that he had said. And Moses chose able men out of all Israel, and made them heads over the people: rulers of thousands, rulers of hundreds, rulers of fifties, and rulers of tens. So they judged the people at all times; the hard cases they brought to Moses, but they judged every small case themselves" (Exodus 18:17-18, 24-26).

"And the LORD said to Moses: "Take Joshua the son of Nun with you, a man in whom is the Spirit, and lay your hand on him; set him before Eleazer the priest and before all the congregation, and inaugurate him in their sight. And you shall give some of your authority to him, that all the congregation of the children of Israel may be obedient." (Numbers 27:18-20)

On the other hand, we see that Joshua was a good example of a leader who was able to work under delegated authority as well as delegate his own authority but he lacked in the area of his understanding of preparing his successor because he didn't have one.

"Now after the death of Joshua it came to pass that the children of Israel asked the LORD, saying, "Who shall be first to go up for us against the Canaanites to fight against them?" (Judges 1:1)

Notice that the children of Israel asked the Lord-not an appointed, designated leader as in times past who would receive the plan and instruction from God and delegate it. If a leader wants to leave a legacy in regards to his or her ministry it is very important that he or she as the senior pastor mentors and grooms a successor.

God gave me revelation a few years back that leaders are DOORS. Jesus said, *"I am the door. If anyone enters by Me, he will be saved, and will go in and out and find pasture" (John 10:9).* Leaders are ultimately the ones that can allow things to come into or go out of that ministry because of the influence they have. In essence, everything that leaders do will in some way affect that ministry or organization.

Notes and Personal Reflection:

_____

_____

_____

_____

_____

_____

_____

_____

_____

_____

_____

_____

_____

_____

_____

SELF – ASSESSMENT

1. As a leader, is it becoming easier or more difficult to get people to follow you?

2. Would you follow yourself?

3. Are there five people within your ministry that respect you and will follow you?
Yes or No

   If so, list their names below:

   1. _____

   2. _____

   3. _____

   4. _____

   5. _____

4. Have you had more than three incidents with individuals in your ministry within the last six months? Yes or No.

5. Have you received three or more compliments on how well you've treated individuals in your ministry within the last six months? Yes or No.

6. Are you pleased with the overall leadership and decision making in your ministry? Yes or No.

7. Are you willing to as a leader be used in any needed area of your ministry? Yes or No.

8. On a scale of 1-10, ten being the highest, concerning your overall character as a member of your ministry, would your rating be between 5-9?

LEADERS PLEGDE OF COMMITMENT

I AM JOINED WITH NO THOUGHT OF LEAVING

I Samuel 20: 23 – "May the Lord be between you and me forever."

I Samuel 14:7 – "Do all that is in your heart. Go then; here I am with you, according to your heart."

Romans 8:31 – What then shall we say to these things? If God is for us, who can be against us?

Judges 4:8 – And Barak said to her, "If you will go with me, then I will go; but if you will not go with me, I will not go!"

I Samuel 20:23 – "May the Lord be between you and me forever."

THIS COMMITMENT IS NOT FOR A TIME OR SEASON BUT FOR LIFE.

Reference List

Your Spiritual Gifts Can Help Your Church Grow, C. Peter Wagner © 1979, 1994, 2005 C. Peter Wagner Published by Regal Books

The 21 Most Powerful Minutes in a Leader's Day, John C. Maxwell ©2000 by Maxwell Motivation, Inc. Published by Thomas Nelson, Inc.,

Merriam-Webster Dictionary©2012 Merriam-Webster, Inc.

Contact Information

For speaking engagement requests or additional copies of the book you may visit our website www.powerandlightchurch.org or contact Power and Light Evangelistic Church at 708-331-9834.